Breaking Free of Every Chain:
A Guide to Financial Freedom and Debt-free Living

By: Dr. Michele W. Smith

Copyright © 2024

By Dr. Michele W. Smith

All rights reserved.

No part of this publication may be reproduced, distributed, or transmitted in any form or by any mean, including photocopying, recording, or other electronic or mechanical methods without the written permission of the publisher, except as permitted by U.S. copyright law. For permission requests, contact Dr. Michele W. Smith, 747 E Hathaway Ave., Box 1135, Bronson, FL 32621.

Table of Contents

INTRODUCTION – SUMMARY..5

CHAPTER 1 - UNDERSTANDING FINANCIAL FREEDOM........................10

CHAPTER 2 - THE ROAD TO DEBT-FREE LIVING....................................14

CHAPTER 3 - FINANCIAL RESPONSIBILITY: LIVING WITHIN YOUR MEANS......19

CHAPTER 4 - MONEY MANAGEMENT:PRINCIPLES OF WEALTH BUILDING....28

CHAPTER 5 - PREPARING FOR RETIREMENT: SECURING YOUR FUTURE.........36

CHAPTER 6 - LIVING DEBT-FREE: EMBRACING PEACE AND CHARITY..............46

CHAPTER 7 - BIBLICAL WISDOM ON DEBT AND FINANCIAL STEWARDSHIP...57

CHAPTER 8 - TESTIMONY: DR. SMITH'S ROAD TO FINANCIAL FREEDOM........64

Introduction

In "Breaking Free of Every Chain," Dr. Michele W. Smith presents a comprehensive roadmap to financial freedom and debt-free living. Drawing from her diverse background as an entrepreneur, accountant, US Navy Veteran, mother, wife, and Christian woman, Dr. Smith combines proven principles, practical strategies, and timeless wisdom to empower readers to take control of their finances and transform their lives.

Understanding Financial Freedom

The journey to financial freedom begins with a clear understanding of its significance. Dr. Smith defines financial freedom as the ability to make choices about how you live your life without being constrained by financial concerns. By exploring the importance of financial independence and the detrimental effects of debt, readers gain insight into why achieving financial freedom is essential for living a fulfilling life.

The Road to Debt-Free Living

Becoming debt-free is not just a goal; it's a tangible reality that anyone can achieve with the right mindset and strategies. Dr. Smith guides readers through practical steps for assessing their current financial situation, creating a realistic budget, and implementing strategies for paying off debt. By adopting proven methods such as the debt snowball and debt avalanche, readers gain the tools they need to break free from the shackles of debt and reclaim control of their financial future.

Financial Responsibility: Living Within Your Means

Living within your means is a cornerstone of financial stability and long-term success. In this chapter, Dr. Smith explores the dangers of living above your means and the importance of delayed gratification. By learning to differentiate between needs and wants and prioritizing financial stability over fleeting indulgences, readers cultivate the mindset of financial responsibility essential for achieving lasting financial freedom.

Money Management: Principles of Wealth Building

Effective money management is crucial for achieving financial freedom and building long-term wealth. Dr. Smith shares essential principles for saving, investing, and achieving financial security. From setting financial goals to building an emergency fund and investing in low-risk opportunities for long-term growth, readers gain practical insights into how to manage their money wisely and build a solid financial foundation for the future.

Preparing for Retirement: Securing Your Future

Retirement planning is a critical aspect of financial freedom and long-term financial security. Dr. Smith provides invaluable guidance on understanding retirement accounts, maximizing employer contributions, diversifying investments, and adjusting retirement plans over time. By taking proactive steps to prepare for retirement, readers can ensure a comfortable and secure future for themselves and their loved ones.

Living Debt-Free: Embracing Peace and Charity

Living debt-free is not just about financial freedom; it's about experiencing peace, joy, and generosity in your life. Dr. Smith explores the profound benefits of debt-free living and how it can transform relationships and attitudes towards money. By finding peace in a debt-free life, experiencing the joy of giving, and cultivating gratitude and contentment, readers discover the true abundance and fulfillment that comes from living a life free from financial bondage.

Biblical Wisdom on Debt and Financial Stewardship

As a Christian woman, Dr. Smith draws inspiration from biblical principles on debt and financial stewardship. By exploring what the Bible says about money management and integrating faith into financial decisions, readers gain a deeper understanding of how to align their financial practices with biblical values and experience greater alignment, purpose, and fulfillment in their financial journey.

Testimony: Dr. Smith's Journey to Financial Freedom

In the final chapter, Dr. Michele W. Smith shares her personal testimony of overcoming financial struggles and achieving debt-free living. Through candid insights, valuable lessons learned, and heartfelt encouragement, readers gain inspiration and empowerment to embark on their own journey to financial freedom.

"Breaking Free of Every Chain" is more than just a book; it's a guide to transforming your relationship with money, Breaking Free of Every Chain from debt, and living a life of abundance, purpose, and generosity. Whether you're a seasoned investor or just starting on your financial journey, this book offers practical advice, proven strategies, and timeless wisdom to empower you to take control of your finances and build a brighter future for yourself and your loved ones.

Chapter 1: Understanding Financial Freedom

Financial freedom is not just about having a large bank account; it's about having control over your finances and the ability to live life on your own terms. To understand financial freedom, we must first define it: it's the state of being free from financial worries and constraints, where money is no longer a source of stress but a tool for achieving your goals, dreams and satisfying all needs.

Defining financial freedom

Financial freedom is achieved when your passive income exceeds your expenses, giving you the option to work or not work, and allowing you to live the life you desire without financial constraints. Financial freedom is like reaching a point where you've got more money coming in from things like investments or rental properties than you're spending on everyday stuff like bills, groceries, and fun activities. So, you're not tied down to a job just to cover your basic needs. Instead, you can choose whether to keep working or take a break, and you can afford to do the things you really want without constantly worrying about money. It's basically having enough financial cushion to live the life you've been dreaming of without stressing about finances all the time.

The importance of financial independence

Financial independence provides a sense of security and peace of mind, knowing that you are not dependent on others for your financial well-being. It empowers you to make choices based on what's best for you, rather than what's dictated by financial necessity. Financial independence is like having a safety net that you've built for yourself. It means you're not relying on anyone else to support you financially. So, whether it's unexpected expenses or changes in your life, you've got the resources to handle them without having to lean on family or friends. It's about feeling confident and in control of your own financial situation. With financial independence, you're free to make decisions based on what you truly want and need, rather than feeling forced to do things just to make ends meet. It's all about having the power to live life on your own terms with grace and independence.

Why debt-free living matters

Debt is a major obstacle to financial freedom, as it limits your ability to save, invest, and build wealth. Living debt-free frees up your income, reduces financial stress, and allows you to focus on achieving your financial goals. Living without debt is like taking a weight off your shoulders. When you owe money, whether it's from credit cards, loans, or other sources, it's like carrying around a burden that holds you back from reaching your financial dreams. Being debt-free means you don't have those monthly payments eating away at your income. Instead, you can use that money to save for the future, invest in things that will grow your wealth, or simply enjoy life without worrying about debts hanging over your head. Plus, without the stress of debt, you can focus more on what you want to achieve financially, whether it's buying a home, starting a business, or saving for retirement. It's all about giving yourself the freedom to pursue your goals without being weighed down by debt.

Chapter 2: The Road to Debt-Free Living

Becoming debt-free is a journey that requires commitment, discipline, and perseverance. It begins with a clear understanding of your current financial situation and a willingness to make necessary changes to improve it.

Assessing your current financial situation

Start by gathering all your financial information, including income, expenses, debts, and assets. Create a detailed budget to track your spending and identify areas where you can cut costs and increase savings. Beginning a debt-free lifestyle involves taking a good look at where you stand financially. To get started, gather up all your financial paperwork, like pay stubs, bills, loan statements, and any information about what you own, like your car or savings accounts. Then, dig into the details by creating a budget. This means listing out all your expenses, from rent or mortgage payments to groceries and entertainment. Once you see where your money is going, you can figure out where you might be able to spend less and save more. Maybe it's cutting back on eating out or finding a cheaper phone plan. By getting a clear picture of your finances and making a plan to manage them better, you're taking the first steps toward living without debt.

Creating a realistic budget

A budget is a roadmap to financial success. Allocate your income towards essential expenses, savings, debt repayment, and discretionary spending. Be realistic and flexible, adjusting your budget as needed to accommodate changes in your financial situation. Crafting a budget is like drawing up a detailed plan for your money. You'll want to divide your income into different categories, like things you absolutely need to pay for (like rent or mortgage, utilities, groceries), money to save for the future (like an emergency fund or retirement), any debts you're working to pay off (like credit cards or student loans), and then whatever's left can go toward things you want but don't necessarily need (like eating out or buying new clothes). It's important to be honest with yourself about what you can afford and be willing to adjust your budget if your financial situation changes. Maybe you get a raise at work or unexpected expenses pop up - your budget should be flexible enough to handle those changes without throwing off your whole financial plan. Think of it as a roadmap that guides you toward your financial goals, but one that you can adjust along the way as needed.

Strategies for paying off debt

There are several approaches to paying off debt, including the debt snowball and debt avalanche methods. With the debt snowball method, you pay off your debts from smallest to largest. The debt avalanche method prioritizes debts with the highest interest rates, saving you money on interest over time. When it comes to tackling your debts, there are different strategies you can use, kind of like different tools in a toolbox. Our most popular method is the debt snowball, which allows for the most immediate rewards. With this approach, you start by paying off your smallest debt first, regardless of the interest rate. It's like clearing away the smallest obstacles first, which can give you a sense of accomplishment and motivation to keep going. Once that debt is paid off, you take the money you were putting toward it and apply it to the next smallest debt, and so on; creating a sort of snowball effect that builds momentum as you go along.

Another method is called the debt avalanche. Instead of focusing on the size of the debt, you target the ones with the highest interest rates first. By tackling these high-interest debts early on, you can save money in the long run because you're cutting down on the amount of interest you'll have to pay over time. It's like prioritizing the biggest financial drains first so you can stop them from getting even bigger.

Both methods have their advantages, so it's important to choose the one that works best for your situation and goals. Whether you prefer the quick wins of the debt snowball or the long-term savings of the debt avalanche, the key is to stay focused and consistent as you work toward becoming debt-free.

Chapter 3: Financial Responsibility: Living Within Your Means

Living within your means is essential for achieving and maintaining financial stability. It requires discipline, self-control, and a willingness to prioritize long-term financial goals over short-term gratification.

The dangers of living above your means

Living above your means leads to overspending, debt accumulation, and financial stress. It creates a cycle of dependency on credit and prevents you from building wealth and achieving financial freedom. Living above your means is like trying to keep up with the Joneses even when you can't afford it. When you spend more money than you earn, it's like digging yourself into a financial hole. You might start relying on credit cards or loans to cover your expenses, thinking you'll pay it back later, but that debt can quickly pile up and become overwhelming. Not only does it put you in a tight spot financially, but it also adds a ton of stress to your life.

Instead of feeling secure and in control of your money, you're constantly worrying about how you'll make ends meet.

Living beyond your means creates this cycle where you're always playing catch-up, never able to get ahead financially. It's like running on a treadmill - you're moving, but you're not actually getting anywhere. And while you're stuck in this cycle of debt and overspending, you're missing out on opportunities to build real wealth and achieve financial freedom. Instead of using your money to invest in things that will grow your wealth over time, you're just trying to keep your head above water.

Breaking free from this cycle means making some tough choices and maybe even some sacrifices. It means living within your means, even if that means cutting back on luxuries or making changes to your lifestyle. But in the long run, it's worth it because it puts you on the path to financial stability and freedom. It's about taking control of your finances and your future, rather than letting them control you.

Delayed gratification

Delaying gratification is a sign of maturity and self-discipline. It involves resisting the temptation to make impulsive purchases and instead focusing on long-term goals and priorities. Practice delayed gratification by setting aside money for savings and investments before indulging in discretionary spending.

Delayed gratification is like putting off something fun now in favor of something even better later on. It's all about having the patience and self-control to resist the urge to spend money on impulse buys or immediate pleasures and instead focusing on what's really important to you in the long run. It's kind of like choosing to save up for a dream vacation instead of splurging on fancy dinners every weekend.

Practicing delayed gratification means being strategic about how you use your money. Instead of spending everything you earn right away, you set aside a portion of it for savings and investments before you even think about treating yourself to anything extra. It's like paying yourself first, ensuring that you're building a secure financial future for yourself before spending money on things that are more about instant gratification.

This isn't always easy, especially in a world where we're bombarded with ads and messages telling us to buy, buy, and buy. But by mastering the art of delayed gratification, you're taking control of your finances and your future. You're making choices that align with your long-term goals and priorities, rather than giving in to short-term impulses. And ultimately, that's what sets you up for success in managing your money wisely.

Delayed gratification and maturity are closely intertwined concepts. Maturity involves being able to consider the consequences of our actions and make decisions that serve our long-term well-being rather than just satisfying immediate desires. Delayed gratification is a key indicator of this maturity because it requires the ability to prioritize future goals over instant gratification. It's like recognizing that a small sacrifice now can lead to greater rewards later on. Mature individuals understand the value of patience and self-discipline in achieving success, whether it's in financial matters or other aspects of life. By practicing delayed gratification, we demonstrate our ability to delay short-term pleasures for the sake of more significant long-term gains, reflecting a level of maturity and wisdom in our decision-making process.

Budgeting for needs vs. wants

Distinguish between essential expenses (needs) and discretionary spending (wants) in your budget. Prioritize your needs and allocate a portion of your income towards savings and debt repayment before allocating funds for wants.

When it comes to budgeting, it's crucial to separate the things you absolutely need from the things you simply want. Essential expenses, or needs, are the things you can't live without, like rent or mortgage payments, utilities, groceries, and transportation to work.

Discretionary spending, or wants, on the other hand, are the extras - like eating out at restaurants, buying new clothes, or going to the movies. The key is to prioritize your needs first and make sure they're covered before you even think about spending money on wants. That means setting aside enough money in your budget to cover all your essential expenses, as well as allocating funds for savings and paying off any debts you might have. Once you've taken care of your needs and financial obligations, then you can decide how much, if any, you want to spend on wants. It's all about making sure your financial house is in order before you indulge in non-essential purchases.

When considering discretionary spending, it's essential to keep your financial priorities in check. Before splurging on wants, it's crucial to ask yourself, "Do I really need this, or am I making a frivolous financial decision?" This simple question can help you differentiate between genuine needs and impulsive wants. Additionally, it's vital to recognize that your wants should never take precedence over more significant financial goals, such as building emergency funds or saving for your children's college education. While indulging in occasional luxuries can add enjoyment to life, it's important to ensure that these purchases align with your overall financial plan. Prioritizing essentials and long-term financial objectives over immediate gratification is a hallmark of responsible money management. By maintaining this perspective, you can strike a balance between satisfying your desires and securing your financial future.

Recognizing and avoiding lifestyle inflation

Lifestyle inflation occurs when your spending increases as your income rises. Avoid lifestyle inflation by maintaining a frugal mindset, resisting the urge to upgrade your lifestyle with every pay raise, and focusing on long-term financial goals. Recognizing and steering clear of lifestyle inflation is crucial for maintaining financial stability and reaching your goals. Lifestyle inflation happens when you start spending more money just because you're earning more. It's like upgrading your car, moving to a fancier apartment, or dining out at expensive restaurants more frequently simply because you got a raise or landed a higher-paying job. While it's natural to want to enjoy the fruits of your labor, succumbing to lifestyle inflation can quickly derail your financial progress.

To avoid lifestyle inflation, it's essential to cultivate a frugal mindset and resist the temptation to upgrade your lifestyle with every increase in income. Instead of automatically spending more as you earn more, focus on your long-term financial objectives. Ask yourself if those extra expenses align with your goals or if they're just temporary pleasures that might hinder your progress in the long run.

One effective strategy is to maintain your current standard of living even as your income grows. This means continuing to live within your means and allocating any extra income towards savings, investments, or paying off debts faster. By avoiding unnecessary increases in spending, you can make significant strides towards achieving financial security and reaching your long-term goals. Remember, it's not about depriving yourself of enjoyment but rather about making intentional choices that support your financial well-being over the long haul.

Chapter 4: Money Management: Principles of Wealth Building

Effective money management is the cornerstone of wealth building and financial freedom. It involves setting clear financial goals, creating a plan to achieve them, and consistently monitoring and adjusting your finances to stay on track.

The importance of saving and investing

Saving and investing are critical for building wealth and achieving financial independence. Start by establishing an emergency fund to cover unexpected expenses, then focus on long-term investments such as retirement accounts, stocks, bonds, and real estate. Understanding the significance of saving and investing is key to securing your financial future. Saving involves setting aside money for future needs or emergencies, while investing is about putting your money into vehicles that have the potential to grow over time, like stocks, bonds, or real estate.

One crucial step in financial planning is establishing an emergency fund. This fund acts as a safety net, providing you with a cushion to fall back on when unexpected expenses arise, such as medical bills or car repairs. Aim to save enough to cover at least three to six months' worth of living expenses in your emergency fund.

Once you have your emergency fund in place, it's time to focus on long-term investments. Retirement accounts, like 401(k)s or IRAs, offer tax advantages and are designed to help you save for retirement. By contributing to these accounts regularly, you're not only preparing for your future but also taking advantage of compound interest, which can significantly boost your savings over time.

Beyond retirement accounts, consider investing in stocks, bonds, or real estate to further diversify your portfolio and potentially increase your wealth. Stocks offer the opportunity for growth, while bonds provide stability and income. Real estate can generate rental income and appreciate in value over time.

The key to successful saving and investing is consistency and patience. Start early, contribute regularly, and stay focused on your long-term goals. While saving and investing require discipline and sacrifice in the short term, they are essential steps toward achieving financial independence and securing a comfortable future for yourself and your loved ones.

Setting financial goals

Define your short-term and long-term financial goals, such as paying off debt, buying a home, saving for retirement, or starting a business. Break down each goal into smaller, actionable steps and create a timeline for achieving them. Setting financial goals is like creating a roadmap for your money, guiding you toward the things you want to achieve in life. These goals can range from short-term targets like paying off debt or saving for a vacation to long-term aspirations such as buying a home, retiring comfortably, or starting your own business.

To get started, it's crucial to clearly define each of your goals. Be specific about what you want to accomplish and why it's important to you. For example, if your goal is to buy a home, consider factors like location, size, and budget. Understanding the details of your goals will help you stay motivated and focused on achieving them.

Once you've defined your goals, break them down into smaller, more manageable steps. This makes them less daunting and easier to tackle. For instance, if your goal is to pay off debt, you might break it down into steps like creating a budget, prioritizing debts, and making extra payments whenever possible.

Creating a timeline for each goal is also essential. Determine when you want to achieve each goal and work backward to identify the steps you need to take along the way. This helps you stay on track and measure your progress over time.

Remember, financial goals aren't set in stone. Life is full of unexpected twists and turns, so it's okay to adjust your goals as needed. The important thing is to stay flexible, stay focused, and keep moving forward, one step at a time, toward a brighter financial future.

Building an emergency fund

An emergency fund provides a financial safety net to cover unexpected expenses, such as medical bills, car repairs, or job loss. Aim to save enough to cover 6-12 months of living expenses in a high-yield savings account or other liquid assets. Building an emergency fund is like creating a financial cushion for life's unexpected curveballs. It's there to catch you when you're hit with unexpected expenses, like a sudden medical bill, car repair, or even if you lose your job. The goal is to save up enough money to cover your living expenses for a certain period, usually around 6 to 12 months. This way, you're prepared for whatever comes your way without having to rely on credit cards or loans, which can lead to more financial stress down the line.

When it comes to where to stash your emergency fund, it's best to keep it in a place where it's easily accessible in case you need it in a hurry. High-yield savings accounts are a popular choice because they offer higher interest rates than traditional savings accounts, allowing your money to grow over time while still being readily available when you need it. Other liquid assets, like certificates of deposit (CDs) or money market accounts, are also options to consider, but make sure you can access your funds without facing penalties or fees.

The key to building an emergency fund is consistency. It's not something you can build overnight, but rather something you contribute to regularly over time. Even if you can only set aside a small amount each month, every little bit adds up and brings you closer to your goal of financial security and peace of mind.

Investing in low-risk opportunities for long-term growth

Diversify your investment portfolio to minimize risk and maximize returns. Consider low-risk investment options such as index funds, mutual funds, exchange-traded funds (ETFs), and bonds, which offer steady returns over time with less volatility. Investing in low-risk opportunities for long-term growth is like planting seeds in a garden that you know will yield a harvest, albeit steadily and predictably. Diversifying your investment portfolio means spreading your money across different types of investments to reduce the risk of losing it all if one investment performs poorly. Think of it as not putting all your eggs in one basket.

Low-risk investment options are like the sturdy, reliable plants in your garden that require minimal maintenance but still yield consistent results over time. Index funds, for example, track the performance of a specific market index, like the S&P 500, and offer broad exposure to a diverse range of stocks. Mutual funds pool money from many investors to invest in a variety of assets, managed by professional fund managers. Exchange-traded funds (ETFs) are similar to index funds but trade on stock exchanges like individual stocks. Bonds, on the other hand, are like loans you give to governments or companies in exchange for regular interest payments and the return of your initial investment when the bond matures.

These low-risk investments may not offer the highest returns compared to riskier options like individual stocks or real estate, but they provide steady growth over the long term with less volatility. They're like the slow and steady growers in your garden that reliably produce fruit season after season. By incorporating these low-risk opportunities into your investment portfolio, you can build wealth steadily and confidently, knowing that your money is working for you while minimizing the ups and downs of the market.

Chapter 5: Preparing for Retirement: Securing Your Future

Retirement planning is essential for ensuring a comfortable and secure future. It requires careful consideration of your financial needs, goals, and timeline, as well as a strategic approach to saving and investing for retirement.

Understanding retirement accounts

Familiarize yourself with different retirement accounts, such as 401(k), IRA, Roth IRA, and employer-sponsored plans. Take advantage of employer contributions and tax benefits to maximize your retirement savings.

Understanding retirement accounts is like learning about different tools you can use to build your financial future, specifically for your retirement years. These accounts come with various benefits and rules, so it's essential to get to know them to make the most of your retirement savings.

The 401(k) is a retirement account offered by many employers, allowing you to contribute a portion of your paycheck to the account before taxes are taken out. Some employers even match a percentage of your contributions, which is essentially free money added to your retirement savings. The money you contribute grows tax-deferred until you withdraw it in retirement.

Individual Retirement Accounts (IRAs) are retirement accounts you can open on your own through banks, brokerage firms, or other financial institutions. There are traditional IRAs, where your contributions may be tax-deductible, and earnings grow tax-deferred until you withdraw them in retirement. Then there's the Roth IRA, where you contribute after-tax dollars, but withdrawals in retirement are tax-free, including any earnings.

Employer-sponsored plans, like 403(b) or 457 plans, are similar to 401(k)s but are offered by specific employers, such as nonprofit organizations or government agencies. These plans often come with similar tax benefits and employer contributions, helping you save more for retirement.

By familiarizing yourself with these retirement accounts, you can take advantage of the tax benefits and employer contributions they offer to maximize your retirement savings. It's like choosing the right tools for the job, ensuring you're building a strong financial foundation for your retirement years.

Taking loans against your retirement accounts to make purchases might seem like a quick solution to financial needs, but it often comes with significant drawbacks. When you borrow from your retirement savings, you're essentially borrowing from your future self. Not only do you miss out on potential investment gains on the borrowed funds, but you also jeopardize your long-term financial security. By withdrawing money from your retirement accounts prematurely, you're not only reducing the amount of money available to grow over time but also potentially incurring taxes and penalties on the withdrawn amount. Additionally, taking loans against your retirement accounts can disrupt your savings discipline and delay your progress toward achieving your retirement goals. It's like robbing Peter to pay Paul - you may solve an immediate problem, but you're ultimately sacrificing your future financial well-being.

Instead of dipping into your retirement savings prematurely, consider other options for meeting your financial needs, such as building an emergency fund or adjusting your budget. By preserving and consistently contributing to your retirement accounts, you're stacking the odds in your favor to become a retired millionaire, enjoying the benefits of compound interest and long-term growth potential.

Maximizing employer contributions

If your employer offers a matching contribution to your retirement plan, contribute enough to receive the full match. This is essentially free money that can significantly boost your retirement savings over time. Maximizing employer contributions to your retirement plan is like seizing a golden opportunity to supercharge your savings. Many employers offer to match a portion of their employees' contributions to retirement accounts, such as a 401(k) or 403(b) plan. This means that for every dollar you contribute, your employer will chip in a certain amount as well, up to a specified limit. It's essentially free money on the table, and failing to take advantage of it is like leaving cash on the ground.

Let's break it down: Say your employer offers a 50% match on contributions up to 6% of your salary. If you earn $50,000 a year and contribute 6% of your salary, or $3,000, your employer will add another $1,500 to your retirement account. That's an instant 50% return on your investment, with no risk involved. Over time, these employer contributions can add up significantly and have a major impact on your retirement savings.

By contributing enough to your retirement plan to receive the full employer match, you're essentially giving yourself a raise - one that goes straight into your retirement savings. It's one of the easiest and most effective ways to boost your retirement savings without any extra effort on your part. So, if your employer offers a matching contribution, be sure to take full advantage of it. It's like having a generous benefactor helping you build your financial future, one contribution at a time.

Diversifying investments for retirement

Invest your retirement savings in a diverse range of assets, including stocks, bonds, real estate, and alternative investments. Diversification helps spread risk and maximize returns, ensuring a stable and secure retirement income. Diversifying your investments for retirement is like building a strong and sturdy house using a variety of materials. Instead of relying on just one type of investment, like stocks, you spread your money across different asset classes, such as stocks, bonds, real estate, and alternative investments. Each of these investments behaves differently under various economic conditions, so by diversifying, you're essentially spreading out your risk.

Imagine you're building a house. You wouldn't want to use only one type of material, like wood, for everything, because if something happens to that material, your entire house could be compromised. Similarly, if you put all your retirement savings into one type of investment, like stocks, and the market takes a downturn, you could lose a significant portion of your savings.

By diversifying your investments, you're like a smart builder who uses different materials strategically. Stocks offer the potential for high returns but come with higher risk. Bonds provide stability and income but may offer lower returns. Real estate can generate rental income and appreciate in value over time. Alternative investments, like commodities or private equity, offer unique opportunities for diversification.

Overall, diversification helps spread risk and maximize returns over the long term. It's like having a safety net underneath you, ensuring that even if one part of your investment portfolio falters, the rest can help cushion the blow. By diversifying your retirement savings, you're building a solid foundation for a stable and secure retirement income, regardless of what the market throws your way.

Adjusting retirement plans over time

Review and adjust your retirement plans regularly to account for changes in your financial situation, goals, and market conditions. Consider working with a financial advisor to develop a personalized retirement strategy tailored to your needs and objectives.

Adjusting your retirement plans over time is like fine-tuning a musical instrument to ensure it plays harmoniously. Just as a musician makes adjustments to produce the best sound, you should regularly review and tweak your retirement plans to ensure they align with your evolving financial situation, goals, and the ever-changing market conditions.

Think of it as navigating a ship through changing seas. You wouldn't set a course and then forget about it - you'd constantly monitor your progress and make adjustments as needed to reach your destination safely and efficiently.

Start by reviewing your retirement plans regularly, perhaps annually or whenever significant life events occur, like a job change, marriage, or the birth of a child. Take stock of your financial situation, including your savings, investments, and any changes in income or expenses. Consider how your goals and priorities may have shifted over time and whether your retirement plans need to be adjusted accordingly.

Market conditions also play a role in shaping your retirement plans. Economic downturns, inflation, and changes in interest rates can all impact the performance of your investments and the amount of income you'll have in retirement. Be prepared to adapt your plans in response to these changes to ensure your financial security.

Working with a financial advisor can be invaluable in developing and refining your retirement strategy. An advisor can help you assess your current situation, identify your goals, and create a personalized plan tailored to your needs and objectives. They can also provide guidance and expertise to help you navigate complex financial decisions and stay on track toward a secure and comfortable retirement.

Ultimately, adjusting your retirement plans over time is essential for staying on course toward your retirement goals. By regularly reviewing and fine-tuning your plans, you can ensure that they remain relevant and effective in helping you achieve the retirement lifestyle you desire.

Chapter 6: Living Debt-Free: Embracing Peace and Charity

Living debt-free is more than just a financial goal; it's a lifestyle choice that brings peace, freedom, and fulfillment. It allows you to focus on what truly matters in life, such as relationships, personal growth, and making a positive impact on others.

Finding peace in a debt-free life

Living debt-free frees you from the burden of financial stress and uncertainty, allowing you to enjoy peace of mind and emotional well-being. It provides a sense of security and stability, knowing that you are in control of your finances and prepared for whatever the future may hold. Finding peace in a debt-free life is like lifting a heavy weight off your shoulders and feeling the relief wash over you. Imagine not having to worry about looming bills or mounting debt payments every month. Living without debt means you're no longer shackled by financial stress and uncertainty. Instead, you're free to enjoy life with a clear mind and a lighter heart.

When you're debt-free, you have a sense of security and stability that comes from being in control of your finances. You're not constantly living paycheck to paycheck or scrambling to make ends meet. Instead, you have the peace of mind of knowing that you have a solid financial foundation to weather any storms that may come your way.

Being debt-free isn't just about the numbers on your bank statement; it's also about your emotional well-being. Without the weight of debt dragging you down, you can focus on what truly matters in life - spending time with loved ones, pursuing your passions, and building a future filled with possibility. It's about living with intention and purpose, knowing that you're making choices that align with your values and goals.

In short, finding peace in a debt-free life is about reclaiming your freedom and taking control of your financial destiny. It's a journey worth embarking on, and the rewards are not just financial - they're emotional and psychological as well. By living debt-free, you're opening yourself up to a world of possibilities and paving the way for a brighter, more fulfilling future.

Living debt-free not only impacts your financial and emotional well-being but can also have a profound effect on your spiritual life. When you're not weighed down by the burden of debt, you have the mental and emotional space to focus on things that truly matter, including your spiritual growth and connection.

Imagine being able to approach your spiritual journey with a clear mind and an open heart, free from the distractions and worries that often accompany financial struggles. Living debt-free allows you to prioritize activities that nurture your spirit, such as meditation, prayer, or spending time in nature, without the constant stress of financial obligations looming over you.

Moreover, being debt-free opens up opportunities for generosity and service, which are core principles in many spiritual traditions. Without the constraints of debt, you can more freely give of your time, resources, and talents to support causes you believe in and help those in need. This sense of abundance and generosity can deepen your spiritual connection and bring greater fulfillment and purpose to your life.

Walking in peace and joy becomes more attainable when you're not weighed down by financial worries. Living debt-free allows you to experience a sense of freedom and contentment that transcends material possessions and external circumstances. You can approach life with gratitude and optimism, knowing that you have the resources and resilience to navigate whatever challenges come your way.

In essence, living debt-free creates space for spiritual growth and fulfillment, enabling you to walk a path of peace, joy, and abundance. It's not just about achieving financial freedom; it's about aligning your financial decisions with your values and priorities, ultimately leading to a more meaningful and purposeful life.

The joy of giving and helping others

Living debt-free enables you to be more generous and charitable, as you have the resources to support causes and organizations that are meaningful to you. Giving back not only benefits others but also brings joy, fulfillment, and a sense of purpose to your own life. The joy of giving and helping others is like filling your heart with warmth and light, radiating positivity and goodwill to those around you. When you're living debt-free, you have the freedom and flexibility to be more generous and charitable, using your resources to support causes and organizations that resonate with you on a personal level.

Imagine being able to contribute to a cause you're passionate about, whether it's supporting education, fighting hunger, or protecting the environment, without worrying about how it will impact your own financial stability. Living debt-free means you have the financial capacity to make a difference in the world, no matter how big or small.

Giving back isn't just about helping others; it's also about enriching your own life in profound ways. When you give to others, whether through donations, volunteering, or acts of kindness, you experience a sense of joy, fulfillment, and purpose that money can't buy. Knowing that you've made a positive impact on someone else's life fills you with a sense of satisfaction and contentment that extends far beyond material wealth.

Moreover, giving back fosters a sense of connection and community, bringing people together in shared purpose and goodwill. It strengthens bonds and builds bridges between individuals and communities, creating a ripple effect of positive change that extends far beyond the initial act of giving.

In essence, the joy of giving and helping others is a powerful force that not only benefits those in need but also enriches your own life in countless ways. When you're debt-free, you have the opportunity to tap into this joy and make a meaningful difference in the world, leaving a legacy of generosity, compassion, and kindness that will endure for generations to come.

Charity and giving encompass far more than just monetary donations; they also include the invaluable gifts of time, knowledge, and expertise. While financial contributions are undoubtedly important, giving back in other ways can be equally impactful and meaningful.

Imagine volunteering your time at a local shelter, mentoring a young person in need, or sharing your skills and expertise to help others succeed. These acts of generosity not only make a tangible difference in people's lives but also create lasting connections and foster a sense of community.

Teaching and sharing knowledge are also powerful forms of giving. Whether you're offering guidance to someone starting their career, sharing your expertise in a particular field, or providing mentorship to a budding entrepreneur, you're helping others grow and succeed. By passing on your knowledge and experience, you're empowering others to reach their full potential and make a positive impact in their own lives and communities.

In essence, charity and giving extend far beyond monetary donations; they encompass the countless ways we can support and uplift one another, from lending a listening ear to sharing our time, skills, and knowledge. By embracing a spirit of generosity in all its forms, we can create a more compassionate and connected world where everyone has the opportunity to thrive.

How debt freedom improves relationships

Debt can strain relationships and create tension between partners, family members, and friends. Living debt-free fosters open communication, trust, and cooperation, strengthening personal and professional relationships and enhancing overall well-being. Debt freedom isn't just about numbers on a balance sheet; it has a profound impact on the quality of our relationships with others. Picture this: debt can be like a heavy cloud looming over relationships, casting a shadow of stress and tension. It's not uncommon for financial struggles to strain partnerships, cause dire stress in marriages, cause conflicts among family members, or even create rifts between friends.

Now, imagine the relief and freedom that come with living debt-free. Without the burden of debt weighing them down, individuals are often more open, honest, and transparent about their financial situations. This fosters healthier communication, deeper trust, and greater cooperation within relationships. Partners can work together as a team to achieve common financial goals, while family members and friends can support each other in making wise financial decisions.

Living debt-free also reduces the financial stress that can often spill over into other areas of life, improving overall well-being and creating a more positive environment for relationships to thrive. Instead of worrying about making ends meet or dealing with mounting debt payments, individuals can focus their energy on nurturing meaningful connections, pursuing shared interests, and enjoying quality time together.

Moreover, the benefits of debt freedom extend beyond personal relationships to professional ones as well. Employees who are financially secure and free from debt-related stress are often more focused, productive, and engaged in their work. This can lead to better performance, stronger teamwork, and enhanced collaboration in the workplace.

In essence, debt freedom isn't just a financial milestone; it's a catalyst for building stronger, healthier, and more fulfilling relationships. By freeing ourselves from the shackles of debt, we create space for deeper connections, greater trust, and enhanced well-being, enriching not only our own lives but also the lives of those we care about. Cultivating gratitude and contentment: Living within your means and embracing a debt-free lifestyle encourages gratitude, contentment, and appreciation for what you have. Instead of constantly chasing material possessions and external validation, focus on cultivating inner peace, happiness, and fulfillment in your life.

Chapter 7: Biblical Wisdom on Debt and Financial Stewardship

The Bible offers timeless wisdom and guidance on debt, money management, and financial stewardship. By aligning our financial practices with biblical principles, we can experience greater financial freedom, abundance, and blessing in our lives.

What the Bible says about debt

The Bible warns against the dangers of debt and encourages us to live within our means, avoid excessive borrowing, and prioritize financial stewardship. Proverbs 22:7 states, "The rich rule over the poor, and the borrower is slave to the lender."

The Bible offers timeless wisdom on managing finances, emphasizing the importance of responsible stewardship and cautioning against the pitfalls of debt. It urges individuals to live within their means, avoiding the temptation of excessive borrowing that can lead to financial bondage and hardship.

Proverbs 22:7 succinctly captures this principle, stating, "The rich rule over the poor, and the borrower is slave to the lender." This verse highlights the inherent power dynamics at play in the relationship between borrower and lender. When we take on debt, we essentially relinquish a degree of control over our financial lives, becoming beholden to creditors and subjecting ourselves to their terms and conditions.

Moreover, the Bible encourages believers to prioritize financial stewardship, recognizing that all resources ultimately belong to God. By managing our finances wisely and prudently, we honor God's provision and demonstrate faithful stewardship of the resources entrusted to us.

In essence, the biblical teachings on debt serve as a timeless guide for navigating the complexities of financial management. They remind us of the importance of living within our means, avoiding the bondage of debt, and prioritizing responsible stewardship of the resources we've been given. By heeding these principles, we can cultivate financial freedom, honor God with our finances, and experience greater peace and abundance in our lives.

God's promises of provision and abundance

Throughout the Bible, God promises to provide for our needs and bless us abundantly when we honor Him with our finances. Philippians 4:19 assures us, "And my God will meet all your needs according to the riches of his glory in Christ Jesus."

In the Bible, there are numerous promises from God regarding provision and abundance for those who trust in Him with their finances. These promises serve as a source of comfort and assurance, reminding believers that God is faithful to meet their needs and bless them abundantly.

One such promise is found in Philippians 4:19, which declares, "And my God will meet all your needs according to the riches of his glory in Christ Jesus." This verse assures believers that God is not only capable but also willing to provide for all their needs. It emphasizes the abundance of God's resources and His unwavering commitment to caring for His children.

This promise is not a blank check for unlimited wealth, but rather an assurance that God will supply everything necessary for His followers to fulfill their purposes and live according to His will. It's a reminder that God's provision is not limited by earthly circumstances or human limitations but is rooted in His infinite power and grace.

By trusting in God's promises of provision and abundance, believers can find peace and confidence in their financial journey. They can approach financial decisions with faith rather than fear, knowing that God is with them every step of the way and will never leave them lacking. Ultimately, these promises serve as a reminder of God's faithfulness and His desire to bless His children with all good things.

The Christian perspective on money management: As Christians, we are called to be wise stewards of the resources entrusted to us by God. This involves managing our finances with integrity, generosity, and faithfulness, and using our resources to glorify God and further His kingdom.

Integrating faith and finances

Faith and finances are interconnected aspects of our lives, and it's essential to integrate them in a way that honors God and aligns with His principles. By seeking God's guidance, trusting in His provision, and following biblical wisdom, we can experience true financial freedom and fulfillment in our lives.

Integrating faith and finances means recognizing that our beliefs and values should inform how we manage our money. It's about understanding that our financial decisions have spiritual implications and striving to align them with God's principles.

Picture it like this: just as we seek God's guidance in other areas of our lives, such as relationships or career choices, we should also seek His wisdom when it comes to our finances. This involves prayer, reflection, and a willingness to listen for God's direction in our financial decisions.

Trusting in God's provision means acknowledging that ultimately, He is the source of all our resources. It's about surrendering our fears and worries about money and placing our trust in His faithfulness to provide for our needs. This doesn't mean we sit back and do nothing; rather, it means we work diligently and responsibly, knowing that God is with us every step of the way.

Following biblical wisdom in our financial management means basing our decisions on timeless principles found in Scripture. This might include living within our means, avoiding debt, practicing generosity, and being good stewards of the resources God has entrusted to us. By aligning our financial practices with these principles, we can experience true freedom and fulfillment in our lives.

Ultimately, integrating faith and finances is about living out our faith in practical ways, even when it comes to something as seemingly mundane as money management. It's about recognizing that every aspect of our lives, including our finances, is an opportunity to honor God and live according to His will. When we do so, we can experience a deeper sense of purpose, peace, and abundance in our lives.

Chapter 8: Testimony: Dr. Michele W. Smith's Journey to Financial Freedom

Personal testimony of author (Written in first person grammar).

In this final chapter, I want to help my readers to understand where I came from and how I got to this point in my life. Just to be clear, I have made some dramatically stupid decisions when it comes to money and life concurrently. It is amazing how a change of mindset can change your life dramatically.

Roughly 56 years ago, I was born to military parents with the fortune of having highly principled southern maternal grandparents. My Dad, although in the military, had a great entrepreneurial spirit and my mother was a nurse and relentless free spender. Therefore, my siblings and I got a mixed bag of philosophies regarding money management and financial responsibility. And yes, we were all moving in strange directions as adults.

Fast forward to my teenage years when I decided that I could go to school and work 2 jobs and then 3 jobs. It was definitely an adventure. I was determined to be able to spend what I wanted, be fake-frugal and save money, all at the same time. The stress was great while I was in high school. After high school, I went to college and acquired an associate's degree in Nursing, which was not my calling and then off to the US Navy. I felt like I was on a path to honor my Mom, who was a nurse and my Dad who was in the Army.

My entire military career, I continued my education until I received 2 bachelor's degrees, an MBA, a doctorate and a PhD. Somewhere along in there, I got married, had a kid and left the military to start my civilian career. All of my degrees except the first one are in accounting where I have my passion. My personality is very static and logical; therefore accounting fit me like a glove. But in the course of my preparation for life, I acquired $250,000 in student loan debt, $35,000 in credit card debt and $10,000 in consumer loan debt. Now, I was ready to get yet another loan to buy our house. Let me just add, that I was introduced to payday loans in the military and made it a point to utilize these often to make payments.

What a great start to our young family life. After adding another $97,000 for our first house, I landed my first position as a staff accountant. I had to get a second job as an auditor to afford to make all of our monthly bills. Together, my husband and I made great money, but we were struggling. I could not figure out why this was so tough financially considering our income. I thought I had prepared myself well, but I had so much debt that I felt like we were just not going to make it.

I finally decided to seek more growth in my spiritual life and one day about 5 years in the mess, I had an epiphany that changed my life. I had asked myself out loud, "why" and my answer to myself was clear, "hey stupid girl, you are in this mess because you decided that racking up $392,000 in debt was a good idea. You wanted all of this, well now you got it and your debt-enslaved life is the cost"

After the tears and feeling way down in the dumps, I walked across the street to talk to my grandmother's house. We always believed that they had a lot of money. As a matter of fact, although nobody ever said it, but we thought they were rich. I asked her how they lived so well and they never seemed to worry about money. She told me they do not have a lot of money, but she said, "We are good stewards over what we do have." Well, that is when I found out that they never had a mortgage and they did not believe in having any debt. She told me that they saved up for everything they bought including their house, cars, etc... Needless to say, I was flabbergasted. My next question to her was, "how come you never told us about this?" Her reply was epic and she looked at me with that "grandma" look and said, "We never told you get into all that debt either, but you did it anyway!"

At that point, my mindset starting to change and all I wanted to do was get my family out of debt and begin to enjoy the peace and joy that we were missing out on everyday of our lives. Although, I did not find out until my grandparents had passed away, neither of them ever earned a living wage, but they lived so well, were extremely charitable and had everything that I wanted to have in my life. All of this with zero debt.

By this time, I was a public accountant; therefore I created financial books and managed other people's money every day as a career, but I was not managing my own money. I owned several businesses and ran them pretty well, but could not manage my own personal finances. I finally began running our lives like a business. Creating a super detailed budget showed me that we had no margin in the six figure money that was coming into our home. We were living paycheck to paycheck. The plan was to create a margin by getting rid of things we did not need, cutting back on "desires," and digging into paying off our massive debt.

Of course it was not easy and it took a lot of patience and prayer! The sacrifice was great but well worth it. The most difficult obstacle is learning to say "no" to yourself and your family. But by the grace of God, we learned to management our money with power of delayed gratification. I have never felt so free then when I knew without a doubt where every dollar we earned was going. Every single dollar had a purpose.

After gaining the peace and joy of living debt-free, I had a huge yearning to share my experiences and expertise with other people, especially young people. Currently, I create budgets for others and counsel with them throughout their financial freedom journeys. This is my charitable work in which fulfils my spirit in ways that words cannot describe fully. Of course, I counsel on more than money, such as life obstacles, relationships, careers, education and whatever else my folks need.

The best feeling for me is that those that I have helped over the years stopped calling me "Dr. Smith" and began calling me "Auntie Chele" (*pronounced Shell, short for Michele*). That has made me so proud, loved and more determined to do much more and gain more nieces and nephews than any auntie in history.

In summary, my story has more twists and turns then there is paper to write on, but it is necessary to let my readers know the following:

My journey was difficult, took 15 years and included speed bumps and pauses along the way. Best practices include never forgetting that you are human and that you will make mistakes. You may get down but be determined to never stay down. Live like the seasons and continually bring new life. You must pay attention to your goals, be committed, and never lose your focus for your future.

I understand that wealth is so much more than money. Our prosperity includes health, peace, joy, family, relationships, mental and spiritual wellness. All of these things must be in place for you to be truly wealthy and are all doable with dedication and focus.

At the beginning of your financial responsibility and wealth building journey, you must rebuke your concern for what other people have to say or think about you. Once you decide that you are moving on a new path you will face negativity from the world, but they lose their vote in your life when your focus and mindset changes.

Remember, it is ok to say "no" regularly. After a while people will just understand that you do not care what they think or say and they will be fine with it. If you find that any relationship is strained because of your intent to do better, then it is not a healthy relationship and it is ok to move on.

Lastly, no matter what happens, never stop moving forward. Remember, one foot in front of the other will get you to the door. Amen!

NOTES

Use the following pages to jot down items that you need and or want to further discuss or remember. Make your lists here. Remember to make lists and write down your thoughts. This is a great method for you to communicate with yourself.-

----

----

www.ingramcontent.com/pod-product-compliance
Lightning Source LLC
Chambersburg PA
CBHW070207230526
45471CB00002B/853